A Super Tasty Sirt Diet Cookbook – 2 Books in 1

Lose Weight like a Celebrity and Activate Your Skinny Gene with the 150+ Recipes Included in this Book!

By

Lara Middleton

Sirt Diet Recipes Cookbook

by

Lara Middleton

5

Additionally, the information in the following pages is intended only for informational purposes and should thus be thought of as universal. As befitting its nature, it is presented without assurance regarding its prolonged validity or interim quality. Trademarks that are mentioned are done without written consent and can in no way be considered an endorsement from the trademark holder.

Table of Contents

Breakfast Recipes

Kale Omelet

Preparation time: 5 minutes

Cooking time: 5 minutes

Serving: 1

Ingredients:

3 Eggs

1 small glove Garlic

2 handfuls Kale

Goat cheese or any cheese of your choice

¼ cup sliced onion

2 teaspoons extra virgin olive oil

Directions:

Mince the garlic, and finely shred the kale.

Break the eggs into a bowl, add a pinch of salt. Beat until well combined.

Place a pan to heat over medium heat. Add one teaspoon of olive oil, add the onion and kale, cook for approx. Five minutes, or until the onion has softened and the kale is wilted. Add the garlic and cook for another two minutes.

Add one teaspoon of olive oil into the egg mixture, mix and add into the pan. Use your spatula to move the cooked egg toward the center and move the pan so that the uncooked egg mixture goes towards the edges.

Add the cheese into the pan just before the egg is fully cooked, then leave for a minute.

Nutrition:

Calorie: 339

Carbohydrates: 30 g

Fat: 11 g

Protein: 30 g

Sirtfood Omelet

Preparation time: 5 minutes

Cooking time: 10 minutes

Serving: 1

Ingredients:

3 Medium eggs

2 ounces Sliced streaky bacon

1 ¼ ounces Red endive

1 teaspoon Turmeric

2 tablespoons Parsley (finely chopped)

1 teaspoon extra virgin olive oil - 1 teaspoon

Directions:

Place a nonstick fry pan to heat over medium-high heat. Add the bacon strips into the pan and cook until crispy. Do not add any oil as the bacon has enough fat to cook itself.

Put off the heat and place the bacon on a paper towel to drain any excess fat. Use a kitchen paper to wipe the pan clean.

Break the eggs into a bowl. Add the turmeric, parsley, and endive. Stir thoroughly. Cut the cooked bacon into cubes, add them into the bowl of the egg mixture and stir together.

Heat the olive oil in the frying pan until hot but not smoking. Then add the egg mixture and use a spatula to move it around the pan until the omelet is on an even level.

Reduce the heat and allow the omelet to firm up.

Use the spatula around the edges of the pan and roll up the omelet, or fold it in half.

Serve immediately.

Nutrition:

Calories: 154

15

Total Fat: 12 g

Cholesterol: 313 mg

Sodium: 155 mg

Potassium: 117 mg

Total Carbohydrates: 0.6 g

Protein: 11 g

Turmeric Scrambled Eggs

Preparation time: 10 min

Cooking time: 10 min

Servings: 3

Ingredients:

1 tablespoon Butter

1 handful large spinach

6 Large eggs

Salt & pepper to taste

2 teaspoons Turmeric powder

1 (chopped) large tomato

1 teaspoon Coconut oil

Directions:

Break the eggs into a medium bowl, whisk and add the pepper, salt, and turmeric. Mix together and set aside.

Heat the coconut oil in a small fry pan, add the chopped tomato and cook for about 2 to 3 minutes, until soft.

Add the spinach into the pan and cook for another two minutes. Set aside.

Add the butter into a small nonstick saucepan to melt under medium-low heat, and then add the egg mixture. Use your spatula to push the eggs from side to side across the pan.

Add the tomato and spinach to the pan when the eggs are almost done.

Once the egg is cooked, serve immediately.

Nutrition:

Calories: 208

Total Fat: 19 g

Total Carbohydrates: 31 g

Protein: 25 g

Sugar: 2 g

Fiber: 2 g

Salt: 1.4 g

Parsley Smoothie

Preparation time: 2 minutes

Cooking time: 2 minutes

Servings: 2

Ingredients:

1 cup Flat-leaf parsley

Juice of two lemons

1 (core removed) Apple

1 Avocado

1 cup Chopped kale

1 knob Peeled fresh ginger

1 tablespoon Honey

2 cups cold water

Directions:

Add all the ingredients except the avocado into your blender.

Blend on high until smooth, then add the avocado, then set your blender to slow speed and blend until creamy.

Add a little more iced water if the smoothie is too thick.

Nutrition:

Calories: 75

Total Fat: 1 g

Total Carbohydrates: 20 g

Protein: 1 g

Fiber: 2 g

Sodium: 26 mg

Matcha Overnight Oats

Preparation time: 5 minutes

Cooking time: 5 minutes

Servings: 2

Ingredients:

For the Oats

2 teaspoon Chia seeds

3 oz Rolled oats

1 teaspoon Matcha powder

1 teaspoon Honey

1 ½ cups Almond milk

2 pinches Ground cinnamon

For the Topping

1 Apple (peeled, cored and chopped)

A handful of mixed nuts

1 teaspoon Pumpkin seeds

Directions:

Get your oats ready a night before. Place the chia seeds and the oats in a container or bowl.

In a different jug or bowl, add the matcha powder and one tablespoon of almond milk and whisk with a hand-held mixer until you get a smooth paste, then add the rest of the milk and mix thoroughly.

Pour the milk mixture over the oats, add the honey and cinnamon, and then stir well. Cover the bowl with a lid and place in the fridge overnight.

When you want to eat, transfer the oats to two serving bowls, then top with the nuts, pumpkin seeds, and chopped apple.

Nutrition:

Calories: 300

Total Fat: 14 g

Total Carbohydrates: 37 g

Protein: 10 g

Yogurt with Mixed Berries, Dark Chocolate, and Chopped Walnuts

Preparation time: 2 minutes

Cooking time: 3 minutes

Serving: 1

Ingredients:

2 teaspoons Grated dark chocolate (85% cocoa solids)

1 cup Greek yogurt

1 cup Mixed berries

¼ cup (chopped) Walnuts

Directions:

Add your preferred berries into a serving bowl. Pour the yogurt on top.

Sprinkle with chocolate and walnuts.

Nutrition:

Calories: 70

Total Fat: 0 g

Cholesterol: 5 mg

Sodium: 80 mg

Potassium: 210 mg

Total Carbohydrates: 12 g

Sugars: 8 g

Protein: 5 g

Dark Chocolate Protein Truffles

Preparation time: 10 minutes

Cooking time: 15 minutes

Servings: 8

Ingredients:

¼ cup Coconut oil

¼ cup Vanilla whey protein powder

¼ cup (chopped) Medjool dates

¼ cup Almond milk

2 tablespoon Honey

⅛ Cup Steel-cut oats

1 tablespoon Coconut flour

2 Dark chocolate bars, minimum 85% cacao

Directions:

Mix the protein powder, honey, almond milk, dates, coconut flour, and oats in a bowl, then mold the mixture into eight balls.

Melt the coconut oil and chocolate over medium heat in a pot. Turn off the heat once melted and allow the chocolate to cool for about five to ten minutes. Dip each of the balls into the melted chocolate until well covered.

Place the balls in the freezer to harden.

Nutrition:

Calories: 65

Total Fat: 5 g

Total Carbohydrates: 2 g

Protein: 3 g

Homemade Kale Chips

Preparation time: 10 minutes

Cooking time: 14 minutes

Servings: 2 to 4

Ingredient:

5 ounces Kale (stalks taken off, washed and dried)

½ teaspoon Chili flakes

1 teaspoon Dried garlic granules

½ teaspoon Salt

1 tablespoon Nutritional yeast flakes

1 tablespoon extra-virgin olive oil

Directions:

Heat your oven to 300 degrees F.

Wash the kale clean and dry the leaves very well. Remove the woody stalks and break into bite-size pieces.

Place the kale into a bowl; sprinkle the remaining ingredients plus the olive oil. Use your fingers to massage the ingredients into the kale until well coated.

Place the coated kale into two baking trays, while ensuring that the leaves do not overlap.

Cook for approx. seven minutes, then rotate the tray and cook for another 7 minutes.

Allow to cool a little before you serve.

Nutrition:

Calories: 96.1

Total Fat: 7.3 g

Cholesterol: 0 mg

Sodium: 611.3 mg

Potassium: 296.5 mg

Total Carbohydrates: 7.3 g

Protein: 2.5 g

Refreshing Watermelon Juice

Preparation time: 2 minutes

Cooking time: 2 minutes

Serving: 1

Ingredients:

20g Young kale leaves (stalks removed)

½ Cucumber (peeled, seeds removed and roughly chopped)

250g Watermelon chunks

250g Mint leaves

Directions:

Add all the ingredients into your blender or juicer. Blend and enjoy.

30

Nutrition:

Calories: 76

Total Fat: 0 g

Total Carbohydrates: 17 g

Protein: 1 g

Matcha Granola with Berries

Preparation time: 10 minutes

Cooking time: 15 minutes

Servings: 4

Ingredients:

1 cup Rolled oats

2 tablespoon Coconut oil

½ cup (chopped) mixed nuts

1 tablespoon Pumpkin seeds

1 tablespoon Matcha powder

1 cup (halved or quartered) Strawberries

1 tablespoon Sesame seeds

½ teaspoon Ground cinnamon

3 tablespoons Runny honey

2/3 cup Blueberries

1 ¾ cups Greek yogurt

Directions:

Heat your oven to 325 degrees F. place parchment paper on a baking tray.

Heat the coconut oil under low heat until it melts. Put off the heat and stir in the seeds, nuts, and oats. Add the cinnamon, matcha powder, and honey, then mix thoroughly.

Evenly spread the granola mixture over the lined baking tray and place in the oven to bake for about fifteen minutes, until crisp and toasted – turn it 2 to 3 times.

Remove from the oven to cool, then store in an airtight container. To serve, layer the yogurt in the serving dishes, then add the berries and granola.

Nutrition:

Calories: 490

Total Fat: 25 g

Sodium: 305 mg

Potassium: 507 mg

Total Carbohydrates: 59 g

Fiber: 9 g

Sugar: 24 g

Coffee and Cashew Smoothie

Preparation time: 2 minutes

Cooking time: 5 minutes

Serving: 1

Ingredients:

1 teaspoon Cashew butter

½ glass Chilled cashew

1 teaspoon Tahini

1 (pitted and chopped) Medjool date

1 shot Espresso coffee

½ teaspoon Ground cinnamon

Tiny pinch of salt

Directions:

Add all the ingredients into a high-speed blender. Blend until creamy and smooth.

Nutrition:

Calories: 125

Total Fat: 4 g

Sodium: 32 mg

Fiber: 3 g

Total Carbohydrates: 22 g

Protein: 3 g

Buckwheat Pita Bread Sirtfood

Preparation time: 5 minutes

Cooking time: 20 minutes

Servings: 6

Ingredients:

1 x 8 gram Packet dried yeast

375ml lukewarm water

3 tablespoon extra-virgin olive oil

500 grams Buckwheat flour

1 teaspoon Sea salt

Polenta for dusting

Directions:

Add the yeast in the lukewarm water, mix and set aside for about 10 to 15 minutes to activate.

Mix the buckwheat flour, olive oil, salt, and yeast mixture. Work slowly to make dough. Cover and place in a warm spot for approx. one hour – this is to get the dough to rise.

Divide the dough into six parts. Shape one of the pieces into a flat disc and place between two sheets of a baking paper. Gently roll out the dough into a round pita shape that is approximately ¼-inch thick. Use a fork to pierce the dough a few times, and then dust lightly with polenta.

Heat up your cast iron pan and brush the pan with olive oil. Cook the pita for about 5 minutes on one side, until puffy, and then turn to the other side and repeat.

Fill the pita with your preferred veggies and meat, and then serve immediately.

Nutrition:

Calories: 205

Total Fat: 7 g

Total Carbohydrates: 30 g

Protein: 6 g

No-Bake Apple Crisp

Preparation time: 5 minutes

Cooking time: 5 minutes

Servings: 8

Ingredients:

8 Apples (peeled, cored and chopped)

2 teaspoons Cinnamon (divided)

1 cup Raisins (soaked and drained)

2 tablespoons Lemon juice

1 cup Medjool dates

2 cups Walnuts

⅛ Teaspoon Sea salt

¼ teaspoon Nutmeg

39

Directions:

Add one teaspoon of cinnamon, the raisins, two apples, and the nutmeg into your food processor.

Toss the remaining chopped apples and the lemon juice in a big bowl.

Pour the apple puree over the apples in the bowl and mix well.

Transfer the mixture into a medium-sized baking dish and keep aside.

Add the remaining cinnamon, dates, sea salt, and walnuts into your food processor. Pulse until coarsely grounded. Do not over mix.

Sprinkle the mixture over the apples and use your hands to press down lightly.

Allow to sit for a few hours for the flavor to marinate or serve immediately.

Nutrition:

Calories: 164.2

Total Fat: 6.2 g

Sodium: 59.6 mg

Potassium: 121.0 mg

Total Carbohydrates: 28.3 g

Protein: 2.3 g

Matcha Latte

Preparation time: 2 minutes

Cooking time: 3 minutes

Serving: 1

Ingredients:

1 mug unsweetened rice milk

½ teaspoon Date syrup (optional)

1 teaspoon Matcha powder

Directions:

41

Heat the matcha and milk in a pan and froth it until it gets hot, stir in your preferred sweetener.

Pour into your cup and Enjoy!

Nutrition:

Calories: 85

Total Fat: 5 g

Total Carbohydrates: 8 g

Fiber: 2 g

Sugar: 6 g

Protein: 2 g

Lunch Recipes

Rocket salad with Tuna

Preparation time: 10 minutes

Cooking time: 15 minutes

Servings: 4

Ingredients:

4 slices rustic bread, torn into pieces

4 large tomatoes

2 Tbsp. olive oil

400g tin cannellini beans, drained and rinsed

¼ cup Kalamata olives

2 cups shredded rocket

¼ red onion, sliced finely

85g tin tuna

Dressing

2 tbsp. olive oil

½ tsp. Dijon mustard

1 tbsp. lemon juice

Directions:

Start with setting the oven at 180C. Place the bread slices in braking tray, put olive oil on slices and bake for 10-15 minutes.

To prepare the dressing mix lemon juice, mustard and oil in a jar.

Bring a bowl; add baked bread, onions, beans, tuna, tomatoes and rocket.

Put the dressing over salad and enjoy.

Nutrition:

Calories: 404

Total Fat: 15 g

Total Carbohydrates: 45 g

Protein: 17 g

Sirt Super Salad

Preparation time: 10 minutes

Cooking time: 10 minutes

Serving: 1

Ingredients:

1 3⁄4 ounces (50g) arugula

3 1⁄2 ounces (100g) smoked salmon slices

1 3⁄4 ounces (50g) endive leaves

1⁄2 cup (50g) celery including leaves, sliced

1⁄8 cups (15g) walnuts, chopped

1⁄2 cup (80g) avocado, peeled, stoned, and sliced

1⁄8 cup (20g) red onion, sliced

1 tablespoon extra-virgin olive oil

1 tablespoon capers

1 large Medjool date, pitted and chopped

1/4 cup (10g) parsley, chopped

¼ Juice of lemon

Directions:

Bring a bowl, place large leaves of salad, add all the ingredients one by one in the bowl and stir through the bowl and enjoy.

Nutrition:

Calories: 17

Total Fat: 0.3 g

Sodium: 8 mg

Total Carbohydrates: 3.3 g

Protein: 1.2 g

Strawberry Buckwheat Tabbouleh

Preparation time: 10 minutes

Cooking time: 10 minutes

Serving: 1

Ingredients:

1/3 cup (50g) buckwheat

1/2 cup (80g) avocado

1 tablespoon ground turmeric

1/8 cup (20g) red onion

3/8 cup (65g) tomato

1 tablespoon capers

1/8 cup (25g) Medjool dates, pitted

2/3 cup (100g) strawberries, hulled

3/4 cup (30g) parsley

1 tablespoon extra-virgin olive oil

1 ounce (30g) arugula

½ Juice of lemon

Directions:

Start with cooking the buckwheat by mixing the turmeric according to the instructions of package. Drain and let it cool.

Now, start chopping the tomatoes, capers, onions, avocados, dates and parsley. Mix all of them with already cooked buckwheat.

After that, take the strawberries, slice them and add them in salad.

Garnish the salad on the arugula bed.

Nutrition:

Calories: 69

Total Fat: 5.7 g

Cholesterol: 0 mg

Total Carbohydrates: 3.8 g

Fiber: 1.2 g

Fragrant Asian Hotpot Sirtfood

Preparation time: 10 minutes

Cooking time: 15 minutes

Servings: 2

Ingredients:

1 tsp. tomato purée

1 star anise, crushed (or 1/4 tsp. ground anise)

Small handful (10g) parsley, stalks finely chopped

Small handful (10g) coriander, stalks finely chopped

Juice of 1/2 lime

1/2 carrot, peeled and cut into matchsticks

500ml chicken stock, fresh or made with 1 cube

50g beansprouts

100g firm tofu, chopped

50g broccoli, cut into small florets

100g raw tiger prawns

50g cooked water chestnuts, drained

50g rice noodles, cooked according to packet instructions

1 tbsp. good-quality miso paste

20g sushi ginger, chopped

Directions:

Take a pan and put the parsley stalks, lime juice, tomato purée, coriander stalks, star anise, and chicken stock, let them simmer for 10-12 minutes.

Now add the broccoli, tofu, carrot, water, chestnuts, and prawns, gently mix them and let them cook completely.

Turn off the heat and add in the miso paste and sushi ginger.

Garnish with coriander and parsley leaves and enjoy.

Nutrition:

Calories: 262

Total Fat: 6 g

Total Carbohydrates: 21 g

Protein: 24 g

Coronation Chicken Salad Sirtfood

Preparation time: 5 minutes

Cooking time: 5 minutes

Serving: 1

Ingredients:

75 g Natural yoghurt

1 tsp. Coriander, chopped

Juice of 1/4 of a lemon

1/2 tsp. Mild curry powder

1 tsp. Ground turmeric

6 Walnut halves, finely chopped

100 g Cooked chicken breast, cut into bite-sized pieces

20 g Red onion, diced

1 Bird's eye chili

1 Medjool date, finely chopped

40 g Rocket, to serve

Directions:

Take a bowl, gather the ingredients and mix them in bowl, and serve the salad on the rocket bedding.

Nutrition:

Calories: 111

Total Fat: 1 g

Total Carbohydrates: 8 g

Protein: 18 g

Buckwheat Pasta Salad

Preparation time: 5 minutes

Cooking time: 10 minutes

Serving: 1

Ingredients:

50g cooked buckwheat pasta

Small handful of basil leaves

Large handful of rockets

1/2 avocado, diced

1 tbsp. extra virgin olive oil

20g pine nuts

8 cherry tomatoes, halved

10 olives

Directions:

Take a bowl or a plate, add in all the ingredients, now scatter the pine nuts all over the ingredients and serve.

Nutrition:

Calories: 155

Total Fat: 1 g

Sodium: 252 mg

Total Carbohydrates: 33 g

Fiber: 4.5 g

Sugar: 1.5 g

Protein: 5.7 g

Salmon Sirt Super Salad

Preparation time: 10 minutes

Cooking time: 10 minutes

Serving: 1

Ingredients:

50g chicory leaves

80g avocado, peeled, stoned and sliced

50g rocket

40g celery, sliced

15g walnuts, chopped

100g smoked salmon slices

20g red onion, sliced

1 large Medjool date, pitted and chopped

1 tbsp. capers

Juice ¼ lemons

10g parsley, chopped

1 tbsp. extra-virgin olive oil

10g lovage or celery leaves, chopped

Directions:

Take a large bowl or plate. Put the large salad leave sin the plate. Add in all the ingredients and stir them well, now enjoy and serve.

Nutrition:

Calories: 17

Total Fat: 0.3 g

Sodium: 8 mg

Total Carbohydrates: 3.3 g

Protein: 1.2 g

Sesame Cucumber Salad

Preparation time: 10 minutes

Cooking time: 15 minutes

Servings: 3

Ingredients:

1 lb. Persian cucumbers

2 tbsp. sesame oil

1 tbsp. sesame seeds

1/2 tbsp. lemon juice

Kosher salt

Honey

1/3 c. cilantro, roughly chopped

1 tbsp. low-sodium soy sauce

1 tsp. grated peeled fresh ginger

Chili oil, for serving

Directions:

Take cucumbers and halve each of them lengthwise and, bash it slightly to crush, and then cut each half into 4 to 6 chunks. Transfer those cucumber chunks into a bowl and add 2 tsp. salt. Keep it aside 10 minutes.

In the meantime, add in together, honey, sesame seeds, oil, ginger, soy sauce and lemon juice together.

Rinse the cucumbers and shake off the water as much as possible by transferring them in colander.

Finely, add to the bowl with dressing and toss to combine, and then toss with cilantro. Serve drizzled with chili oil.

Nutrition:

Calories: 36.4

Total Fat: 1.3 g

Sodium: 3.4 mg

Potassium: 249.3 mg

Total Carbohydrates: 5.9 g

Protein: 1.5 g

Cowboy Caviar

Preparation time: 20 minutes

Cooking time: 2 hours

Servings: 5

Ingredients:

1/3 cup lime juice

1 cup fresh corn kernels, from about 2 ears

1 cup fresh corn kernels, from about 2 ears

1/2 cup fresh cilantro, chopped

1 15.5-oz cans black-eyed peas, rinsed

2 scallions, finely chopped

Salt and pepper

1 yellow pepper, finely chopped

1 large jalapeño, finely chopped

1/2 lb. Campari or plum tomatoes, cut into 1/4-inch pieces

1 tbsp. olive oil

Chips, for serving

Directions:

Start with taking a bowl; combine the garlic, salt, oil, lime juice and pepper.

Add in the jalapeno, peas, corn, tomatoes, yellow pepper and scallions.

Keep them in refrigerator for approximately 2 hours.

Garnish with cilantro and avocado and serve.

Nutrition:

Calories: 142.3

Total Fat: 4.9 g

Sodium: 85.4 mg

Potassium: 451.2 mg

Total Carbohydrates: 21.6 g

Protein: 5.7 g

Greek Salad

Preparation time: 10 minutes

Cooking time: 10 minutes

Servings: 4

Ingredients:

3 tbsp. red wine vinegar

2 tsp. confectioners' sugar

Salt and pepper

1 tsp. chopped fresh oregano

8 oz. cucumbers cut into 1/4-in.-thick rounds

1/2 very small red onion, thinly sliced

1/3 cup pitted Kalamata olives, halved

2 tbsp. capers, drained and roughly chopped

1 lb. mixed cherry, grape, and tomatoes (halved or cut into wedges)

2 tbsp. olive oil

Feta cheese, cut into small cubes, for serving

Directions:

Take a bowl; mix together vinegar, oil, sugar, and 1/4 teaspoon each salt and pepper. Stir in capers and oregano.

Now, arrange tomatoes and cucumbers on a platter and scatter onion and olives on top. Spoon dressing over salad and serve the salad with feta.

Nutrition:

Calories: 320

Total Fat: 22 g

Total Carbohydrates: 11 g

Protein: 19 g

Summer Squash Slaw with feta and Toasted Buckwheat

Preparation time: 5 minutes

Cooking time: 10 minutes

Servings: 4

Ingredients:

¼ cup buckwheat groats

2 scallions, thinly sliced

¼ cup coarsely chopped fresh mint

3 tablespoons olive oil

1 tablespoon fresh lemon juice

Salt, freshly ground pepper

1 teaspoon coarsely chopped fresh marjoram or oregano

1½ pounds yellow summer squash, julienned on a mandolin or with a knife

4 ounces feta, thinly sliced

Directions:

Start with toasting the buckwheat in a skillet over medium heat, approximately for 4-5 minutes. Put it to a plate; let it cool.

Add in mint, squash, oil, scallions, lemon juice, marjoram, and oil, sprinkle salt, pepper if you want.

In the end, put in buckwheat and feta and serve.

Nutrition:

Calories: 205

Total Fat: 16 g

Cholesterol: 25 mg

Sodium: 260 mg

Potassium: 19 mg

Total Carbohydrates: 9 g

Protein: 6 g

Buckwheat Noodles with Kimchi and Eggs

Preparation time: 10 minutes

Cooking time: 15 minutes

Servings: 4

Ingredients:

12 oz. Korean buckwheat noodles

1 12-oz. jar napa kimchi

1 tablespoon (or more) sugar

1 tablespoon toasted sesame oil

Salt

2 large eggs, hardboiled, quartered

4 scallions, thinly sliced

½ hot house cucumber, julienned

½ cup thinly sliced toasted laver or nori sheets

2 tablespoons toasted sesame seeds

2 tablespoons (or more) rice wine vinegar

Directions:

Take a large pot of water and boil it. Put noodles and cook, stirring occasionally, until cooked through, but still slightly bouncy, about 1½ minutes.

Drain and rinse under cold running water; put it aside.

Drain kimchi, reserving liquid; chop kimchi. Combine kimchi, kimchi liquid, vinegar, oil, and sugar in a large bowl and toss to combine.

Add the cooked noodles and toss to coat; season with salt and more vinegar or sugar.

Serve the dish with egg, cucumber, scallions, laver, sesame seeds, and 2 cups crushed ice.

Nutrition:

Calories: 511

Total Fat: 12 g

Total Carbohydrates: 89 g

Protein: 17 g

Vegan Buckwheat Risotto

Preparation time: 15 minutes

Cooking time: 15 minutes

Servings: 4

Ingredients:

250ml vegetable stock

1 big bunch of asparagus, chopped

2 cloves of garlic, minced

2 tablespoons macadamia, olive, or coconut oil, divided

1 small white onion, finely chopped

250g buckwheat, soaked overnight + drained and rinsed

1 small white onion, finely chopped

1 tablespoon dried Italian herbs

120g peas, fresh or thawed frozen

Large handful spinach, finely chopped

Salt + pepper

1 lemon, juiced and zested

Handful of parsley, oregano and basil, roughly chopped + more for topping

2 tablespoons nutritional yeast

Extra virgin olive oil, for drizzling

Directions:

Start with preparing veggie stock in a pan and boil them now dim the heat to simmer finely.

Take a large pan, heat 1 tbsp. of oil and fry your asparagus on light heat, until tender but still retains a bite -around 1 minute. Now, remove from the pan and put it aside.

Now, add the remaining oil along with the onion and garlic in the same pan and cook until soft, about 5 minutes. Put buckwheat, dried herbs, apple cider vinegar, and lemon juice to the pan and stir so that every ingredient is finely coated.

Put in veggie stock a little bit at a time, stirring occasionally, just like you would ordinary risotto.

Once the buckwheat is almost fully cooked, stir in your peas and spinach.

Cook more for few minutes then turn off the heat, stir in your herbs, lemon zest, nutritional yeast, salt and pepper. Taste and adjust seasoning, either putting in some more lemon juice or yeast for a cheesier flavour.

Use the asparagus, herbs and olive oil as toppings and serve.

Nutrition:

Calories: 24

Total Fat: 0.02 g

Total Carbohydrates: 0.24 g

Protein: 0.07 g

Miso marinated baked Cod with Stir fried Greens and Sesame seeds

Preparation time: 10 minutes

Cooking time: 15 minutes

Serving: 1

Ingredients:

20g miso

1 tbsp. extra virgin olive oil

1 tbsp. mirin

20g red onion, sliced

200g skinless cod fillet

1 garlic clove, finely chopped

40g celery, sliced

1 tsp. finely chopped fresh ginger

50g kale, roughly chopped

1 bird's eye chili, finely chopped

5g parsley, roughly chopped

60g green beans

1 tbsp. tamari

30g buckwheat

1 tsp. sesame seeds

1 tsp. ground turmeric

Directions:

Firstly, mix the miso, mirin and 1 teaspoon of the oil. Rub all over the cod and leave to marinate for 30 minutes. Now, preheat the oven to 220°C/gas 7.

Start baking the cod for almost 10 minutes.

Meantime heat a pan or wok with the remaining oil. Add the onion and stir-fry for a few minutes, then add the celery, garlic, chili, ginger, green beans and kale. Toss and fry until the kale is tender and cooked through.

Start cooking the buckwheat by following packet instructions with the turmeric for 3 minutes.

Add the sesame seeds, parsley and tamari to the stir-fry and enjoy with the greens and fish.

Nutrition:

Calories: 227

Total Fat: 3 g

Cholesterol: 60 mg

Sodium: 634 mg

Potassium: 30 mg

Total Carbohydrates: 15 g

Protein: 30 g

Dinner Recipes

Red Wine Marinated Grilled Tuna Steaks

Preparation time: 10 minutes

Cooking time: 30 minutes

Servings: 3

Ingredients:

4 (5 ounce) fresh tuna steaks, 1 inch thick

¼ cup soy sauce

½ cup dry red wine

¼ cup extra virgin olive oil

1 tablespoon fresh squeezed lime juice

1 clove garlic, minced

Directions:

Place tuna steaks in a shallow baking dish.

In a medium bowl, mix soy sauce, red wine, olive oil, lime juice, and garlic.

Pour the soy sauce mixture over the tuna steaks and turn to coat.

Cover, and refrigerate for at least one hour.

Preheat grill for high heat.

Lightly oil the grill grate and place tuna steaks on grill, discarding remaining marinade.

Grill for 3 to 6 minutes per side, or to desired firmness.

Nutrition:

Calories: 306

Fat: 8.9 g

Fiber: 11.1 g

Carbohydrates: 23.8 g

Protein: 14.5 g

Matcha Green Tea Salmon

Preparation time: 10 minutes

Cooking time: 20 minutes

Servings: 3

Ingredients:

4 (5 oz.) salmon fillets

2 tablespoons of extra virgin olive oil

2 tablespoons of fresh squeezed lemon juice

1 teaspoon of Matcha green tea powder

½ cup of wholegrain breadcrumbs

Salt and pepper to taste

Directions:

Preheat the oven to 350 degrees F.

79

While the oven is heating, add the olive oil, lemon juice, Matcha green tea powder, wholegrain breadcrumbs, salt and pepper to the large bowl and knead all the ingredients together using your hands.

Place the salmon fillets in the large bowl and cover them each with the breadcrumb mixture, pressing or patting into the fillet as needed. Place salmon fillets on a baking tray and bake them for 20 minutes.

Nutrition:

Calories: 207

Carbohydrates: 31 g

Protein: 5.1 g

Fat: 7 g

Tuscan Garlic Chicken

Preparation time: 10 minutes

Cooking time: 40 minutes

Servings: 3

Ingredients:

2 tablespoons extra virgin olive oil

¼ teaspoon dried parsley

¼ teaspoon dried oregano

¼ teaspoon dried lovage

1 teaspoon garlic powder

½ cup Parmesan cheese

1 cup arugula, chopped

½ cup sundried tomatoes

1/3 cup capers, drained

Directions:

Warm the olive oil in a large pan on medium heat. Add the chicken and cook for 3-5 minutes until brown all over.

When the chicken is no longer pink in the center, remove it from heat and set aside on a plate.

Add the chicken broth, heavy cream, garlic powder, parsley, oregano, lovage, and Parmesan cheese to the pan. Whisk on medium heat until it thickens.

Add the arugula, sundried tomatoes and capers, allowing them to simmer, until the arugula starts to wilt.

Then add the chicken back to the mixture in the pan to reheat for 1 minute before serving.

Nutrition:

Calories: 285

Carbs: 46.2 g

Protein: 8.5 g

Fat: 7.4 g

Baked Walnut Chicken Breast

Preparation time: 10 minutes

Cooking time: 50 minutes

Servings: 3

Ingredients:

¼ cup of walnuts, chopped

2 tbsp. extra virgin olive oil

2 boneless, skinless chicken breasts

Directions:

Preheat the oven to 350 degrees F.

83

Slice a deep groove into the middle of each chicken breast using a sharp knife and place the chopped walnuts in this groove, pouring the olive oil over top.

Put the chicken breasts on a baking tray and bake for 20 minutes.

Nutrition:

Calories: 202

Carbs: 21 g

Protein: 8 g

Fat: 10 g

Roast Duck with Apple Dressing

Preparation time: 10 minutes

Cooking time: 70 minutes

Servings: 3

Ingredients:

1 (4 pound) whole duck

Salt and pepper to taste

1 teaspoon poultry seasoning

2 tablespoon extra-virgin olive oil

3 tablespoons red onion, chopped

5 stalks celery, chopped

3 cups, chopped

3 cups cornbread crumbs

Directions:

85

Preheat oven to 350 degrees F.

Rinse the duck and pat dry. Rub with salt, pepper, and poultry seasoning, to taste.

Heat 1 tablespoon of the olive oil in a small skillet over medium heat. Sauté onion and celery until it tender.

In a medium bowl, combine with apple and cornbread crumbs with the onion-celery mixture.

Mix together to make stuffing, add little water to moisten if necessary. Fill the duck's cavity with the stuffing and sew shut with kitchen twine. Rub the outside of bird lightly with the remaining tablespoon of olive oil, and place in a shallow roasting pan or 9x13 inch baking dish.

Bake in preheated oven for 60 to 80 minutes, or until internal temperature reaches 180 degrees F.

Nutrition:

Calories: 282

Fat: 18.6 g

Fiber: 4 g

Carbohydrates: 9 g

Protein: 18 g

Shrimp Asparagus Alfredo

Preparation time: 10 minutes

Cooking time: 30 minutes

Servings: 3

Ingredients:

1 pound fettuccine noodles, cooked al dente

1 pound shrimp, peeled and deveined

6 tablespoons unsalted butter, divided

6 garlic slice

1 cup heavy cream

1 cup half

1/2 tsp. ground nutmeg

1/3 cup Parmesan cheese

1 cup blanched asparagus, cut into pieces

Parsley

Salt & pepper

Directions:

Season the shrimp with salt.

Melt 3 tbsps. of butter in a large skillet. Shrimp until cooked, then remove the shrimp.

Add the remaining butter to the Pan. Whisk in the cream and nutmeg. Season it with salt and pepper. Garnish with a sprinkle of chopped parsley.

Nutrition:

Calories: 52

Complete Fat 42 g

Immersed Fat 5.8 g

Cholesterol 32 mg

Sodium 25 mg

Potassium 65 mg

Starches 5 g

Chicken Ayam

Preparation time: 10 minutes

Cooking time: 40 minutes

Servings: 3

Ingredients:

1 sliced red chili

1 teaspoon of ginger

1 small red onion, sliced

1 teaspoon turmeric

1 teaspoon galangal

4 cloves of garlic

1 pinch black pepper

3 tips muscovado sugar

3 tsp. shrimp paste

1/3 cup coconut milk

Directions:

Season the chicken legs. Put on low heat on the grill for about 10 min on one side.

Bring all the ingredients together as finely as possible using a mortar and pestle or a blender.

Fry in some peanut oil. Put some paste on the chicken.

Cook the other side for about 5 minutes. Add some glue to the chicken.

Move to the hotter side of the grill, flip, baste and cook for three additional minutes on both sides. Grill the cake on both sides.

Nutrition:

Calories: 41 g

Fat: 2.3 g

Cholesterol: 35mg

Sodium: 75 mg

Potassium: 7g

Starches: 61 mcg

Calcium: 45 mg

Garbanzo Kale Curry

Preparation time: 10 minutes

Cooking Time: 30 minutes

Servings 8

Ingredients:

4 cups dry garbanzo beans

Curry Paste, but go low on the heat

1 cup sliced tomato

2 cups kale leaves

1/2 cup coconut milk

Directions:

Put ingredients in the slow cooker. Cover, & cook on low for 30 minutes.

Nutrition:

Calories: 282

Total Fat: 12.6g

Carbohydrates: 11.5g

Protein: 17.3g

Tomato Frittata

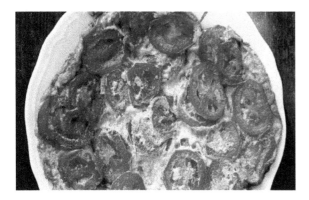

Preparation time: 15 minutes

Cooking time: 20 minutes

Servings: 2

Ingredients:

50g cheddar cheese, grated

75g kalamata olives, pitted and halved

8 cherry tomatoes, halved

4 large eggs

1 tbsp. fresh parsley, chopped

1 tbsp. fresh basil, chopped

1 tbsp. olive oil

Directions:

Whisk eggs together in a large mixing bowl. Toss in the parsley, basil, olives, tomatoes and cheese, stirring thoroughly.

In a small skillet, heat the olive oil over high heat. Pour in the frittata mixture and cook for 5-10 minutes, or set.

Remove the skillet from the hob and place under the grill for 5 minutes, or until firm and set. Divide into portions and serve immediately.

Nutrition:

Calories: 269

Protein: 9.23 g

Fat: 23.76 g

Carbohydrates: 5.49 g

Horseradish Flaked Salmon Fillet & Kale

Preparation time: 15 minutes

Cooking time: 30 minutes

Servings: 2

Ingredients:

200g skinless, boneless salmon fillet

50g green beans

75g kale

1 tbsp. extra virgin olive oil l

½ garlic clove, crushed

50g red onion, chopped

1 tbsp. fresh chives, chopped

95

1 tbsp. freshly chopped flat-leaf parsley

1 tbsp. low fat crème fraiche

1tbsp horseradish sauce

Juice of ¼ lemons

Directions:

Preheat the grill.

Sprinkle a salmon fillet with salt and pepper. Place under the grill for 10-15 minutes. Flake and set aside.

Using a steamer, cook the kale and green beans for 10 minutes.

In a skillet, warm the oil over a high heat. Add garlic and red onion and fry for 2-3 minutes. Toss in the kale and beans, and then cook for 1-2 minutes more.

Mix the chives, parsley, crème fraiche, horseradish, lemon juice and flaked salmon.

Serve the kale and beans topped with the dressed flaked salmon.

Nutrition:

Calories: 206 kcal

Protein: 26.7 g

Fat: 6 g

Carbohydrates: 11 g

Greek Sea Bass Mix

Preparation time: 10 minutes

Cooking time: 22 minutes

Servings: 2

Ingredients:

2 sea bass fillets, boneless

1 garlic clove, minced

5 cherry tomatoes, halved

1 tablespoon chopped parsley

2 shallots, chopped

Juice of ½ lemons

1 tablespoon olive oil

8 ounces baby spinach

Cooking spray

Directions:

Grease a baking dish with cooking oil then add the fish, tomatoes, parsley and garlic. Drizzle the lemon juice over the fish, cover the dish and place it in the oven at 350 degrees F. Bake for 15 minutes and then divide between plates. Heat up a pan with the olive oil over medium heat, add shallot, stir and cook for 1 minute. Add spinach, stir, cook for 5 minutes more, add to the plate with the fish and serve. Enjoy!

Nutrition:

Calories: 210

Fat: 3 g

Fiber: 6 g

Carbohydrates: 10 g

Protein: 24 g

Pomegranate Guacamole

Preparation time: 10 minutes

Cooking Time: 30 minutes

Servings 4

Ingredients:

Flesh of 2 ripe avocados

Seeds from 1 pomegranate

1 bird's-eye chili pepper, finely chopped

½ red onion, finely chopped

Juice of 1 lime

151 calories per serving

Directions:

Place the avocado, onion, chill and lime juice into a blender and process until smooth.

Stir in the pomegranate seeds.

Chill before serving. Serve as a dip for chop vegetables.

Nutrition:

Calories: 127

Carbohydrates: 13 g

Protein: 7 g

Fat: 5 g

Cajun Steak and Veg Rice Jar Recipe

Preparation time: 10 minutes

Cooking time: 25 minutes

Servings: 3

Ingredients:

1 tablespoon vegetable oil

1 celery stick, finely chopped

3 large carrots, sliced into rounds

250g frozen chopped mixed peppers

4 spring onions, chopped, green and white parts split

500g 5 percent beef mince

2 teaspoon seasoning

1 teaspoon tomato purée

2 x 250g packs ready-cooked long-grain rice

Directions:

Heat the oil in a large, shallow skillet over moderate heat. Add the carrots, celery, peppers and frozen peppers. Cook for 10 minutes before the vegetable is beginning to soften.

Insert the mince, season liberally and cook for 10 minutes before mince is browned and start to get crispy.

Add the Cajun seasoning and tomato purée; stir fry to coat the mince. Place with the rice, combined with 4 tablespoons of plain water. Stir to completely combine until the rice is hot. Sprinkle on the rest of the spring onion before serving.

Nutrition:

Calories: 456

Fat: 12 g

Sugar: 13 g

Sodium: 1 g

Carbohydrates: 53 g

Protein: 32 g

Fiber: 8 g

Roast Duck Legs with Red Wine Sauce

Preparation time: 10 minutes

Cooking time: 1 hour

Servings: 3

Ingredients:

1 bunch fresh rosemary, chopped

4 large garlic cloves

4 duck legs

Salt to taste

1 teaspoon Chinese five-spice powder

1 ½ cups red wine

1 ½ tablespoons red currant jelly

Directions:

Preheat an oven to 375 degrees.

Spread the rosemary sprigs and whole garlic cloves into a 9x13-inch baking dish.

Place the duck legs on top of the rosemary, and sprinkle with salt and five-spice powder. Bake in the preheated oven for 1 hour.

Meanwhile, bring the wine to a boil in a small saucepan over medium-high heat. After the duck has cooked 1 hour, pour off and discard the fat that has accumulated in the baking dish. Pour the wine sauce over the duck legs and bake 15 minutes more until the duck is very tender and the sauce has thickened slightly.

Nutrition:

Calories: 282

Total Fat: 10.2 g

Carbohydrates: 8 g

Protein: 15 g

Snacks Recipes

Crunchy Potato Bites

Preparation time: 10 minutes

Cooking time: 20 minutes

Servings: 5

Ingredients:

1 potato, sliced

2 bacon slices, already cooked and crumbled

1 small avocado, pitted and cubed

1 tbsp. of extra virgin olive oil

Directions:

Spread potato slices on a lined baking sheet.

Toss around with the extra virgin olive oil.

Insert in the oven at 350 degrees F.

Bake for 20 minutes.

Arrange on a platter, top each slice with avocado and crumbled bacon and serve as a snack.

Nutrition:

Calories: 230

Total Fat: 14 g

Carbohydrates: 25 g

Protein: 2 g

Sprouts and Apples Snack Salad

Preparation time: 10 minutes

Cooking time: 10 minutes

Servings: 5

Ingredients:

1 pound Brussels sprouts, shredded

1 cup walnuts, chopped

1 apple, cored and cubed

1 red onion, chopped

For the salad dressing:

3 tablespoons red vinegar

1 tablespoon mustard

½ cup olive oil

1 garlic clove, minced

Black pepper to the taste

Directions:

In a salad bowl, mix sprouts with apple, onion and walnuts.

In another bowl, mix vinegar with mustard, oil, garlic, and pepper and whisk really well.

Add the dressing to your salad, toss well and serve as a snack.

Nutrition:

Calories: 46

Total Fat: 2 g

Total Carbohydrates: 6 g

Protein: 2.2 g

Moroccan Snack Salad

Preparation time: 10 minutes

Cooking time: 10 minutes

Servings: 5

Ingredients:

1 bunch radishes, sliced

3 cups leeks, chopped

1 and ½ cups olives, pitted and sliced

A pinch of turmeric powder

Black pepper to the taste

2 tablespoons olive oil

1 cup cilantro, chopped

Directions:

In a bowl, mix radishes with leeks, olives and cilantro.

Add black pepper, oil and turmeric, toss to coat and serve as a snack.

Nutrition:

Calories: 121

Total Fat: 12 g

Total Carbohydrates: 15 g

Protein: 27 g

Celery and Raisins Snack Salad

Preparation time: 10 minutes

Cooking time: 10 minutes

Servings: 3

Ingredients:

½ cup raisins

4 cups celery, sliced

¼ cup parsley, chopped

½ cup walnuts, chopped

Juice of ½ lemons

2 tablespoons olive oil

Salt and black pepper to the taste

Directions:

In a salad bowl, mix celery with raisins, walnuts, parsley, lemon juice, oil, and black pepper and toss.

Divide into small cups and serve as a snack.

Nutrition:

Calories: 267

Total Fat: 11 g

Cholesterol: 1.3 mg

Sodium: 59 mg

Total Carbohydrates: 42 g

Protein: 5 g

Spicy Pumpkin Seeds Bowl

Preparation time: 10 minutes

Cooking time: 20 minutes

Servings: 5

Ingredients:

½ tablespoon chili powder

½ teaspoon cayenne pepper

2 cups pumpkin seeds

2 teaspoons lime juice

Directions:

Spread pumpkin seeds on a lined baking sheet, add lime juice, cayenne and chili powder, and toss well.

Put it in the oven and roast at 275 degrees F for 20 minutes.

Divide into small bowls and serve as a snack.

Nutrition:

Calories: 144

Total Fat: 16 g

Sodium: 75 mg

Potassium: 269 mg

Total Carbohydrates: 5 g

Protein: 11 g

Apple and Pecan Bowls

Preparation time: 10 minutes

Cooking time: 10 minutes

Servings: 4

Ingredients:

4 big apples, cored, peeled and cubed

2 teaspoons lemon juice

¼ cup pecans, chopped

Directions:

In a bowl, mix apples with lemon juice, and pecans and toss.

Divide into small bowls and serve as a snack.

Nutrition:

Calories: 230

Total Fat: 17 g

Total Carbohydrates: 15 g

Cheesy Mushrooms

Preparation time: 10 minutes

Cooking time: 30 minutes

Servings: 5

Ingredients:

20 white mushroom caps

1 garlic clove, minced

3 tablespoons parsley, chopped

2 yellow onions, chopped

Black pepper to the taste

½ cup low-fat parmesan, grated

¼ cup low-fat mozzarella, grated

A drizzle of olive oil

2 tablespoons non-fat yogurt

Directions:

118

Heat up a pan with some oil over medium heat, add garlic and onion, stir, cook for 10 minutes and transfer to a bowl.

Add black pepper, garlic, parsley, mozzarella, parmesan and yogurt, stir well, stuff the mushroom caps with the mix.

Arrange them on a lined baking sheet and bake in the oven at 400 degrees F for 20 minutes.

Serve them as an appetizer.

Nutrition:

Calories: 100

Total Fat: 7 g

Cholesterol: 22.2 mg

Sodium: 202 mg

Potassium: 195 mg

Total Carbohydrates: 2.5 g

Protein: 6 g

Shrimp Muffins

Preparation time: 10 minutes

Cooking time: 45 minutes

Servings: 6

Ingredients:

1 spaghetti squash, peeled and halved

2 tablespoons avocado mayonnaise

1 cup low-fat mozzarella cheese, shredded

8 ounces shrimp, peeled, cooked and chopped

1 and ½ cups almond flour

1 teaspoon parsley, dried

1 garlic clove, minced

Black pepper to the taste

Cooking spray

Directions:

Arrange the squash on a lined baking sheet.

Insert in the oven at 375 degrees F and bake for 30 minutes.

Scrape squash flesh into a bowl and add pepper, parsley flakes, flour, shrimp, mayo, and mozzarella and stir well.

Divide this mix into a muffin tray greased with cooking spray.

Bake in the oven at 375 degrees F for 15 minutes.

Serve them cold as a snack.

Nutrition:

Calories: 321

Total Fat: 16 g

Cholesterol: 49 mg

Sodium: 393 mg

Total Carbohydrates: 35 g

Protein: 9 g

Mozzarella Cauliflower Bars

Preparation time: 10 minutes

Cooking time: 40 minutes

Servings: 12

Ingredients:

1 big cauliflower head, riced

½ cup low-fat mozzarella cheese, shredded

¼ cup egg whites

1 teaspoon Italian seasoning

Black pepper to the taste

Directions:

Spread the riced cauliflower on a lined baking sheet and cook in the oven at 375 degrees F for 20 minutes.

Transfer to a bowl, add black pepper, cheese, seasoning and egg whites, stir well, spread into a rectangle pan and press well on the bottom.

Introduce in the oven at 375 degrees F and bake for 20 minutes.

Let it cool and cut into 12 bars

Serve at room temperature as a snack.

Nutrition:

Total Fat: 5 g

Cholesterol: 33 mg

Sodium: 297 mg

Potassium: 172 mg

Total Carbohydrates: 3.8 g

Fiber: 1.4 g

Protein: 6 g

Cinnamon Apple Chips

Preparation time: 10 minutes

Cooking time: 2 hours

Servings: 4

Ingredients:

Cooking spray

2 teaspoons cinnamon powder

2 apples, cored and thinly sliced

Directions:

Arrange apple slices on a lined baking sheet, spray them with cooking oil, and sprinkle cinnamon on it.

Put it in the oven and bake at 300 degrees F for 2 hours.

Divide into bowls and serve as a snack.

Nutrition:

Calories: 110

Total Carbohydrates: 27 g

Fiber: 4 g

Sugar: 21 g

Vegetable and Nuts Bread Loaf

Preparation time: 15 minutes

Cooking time: 1 hour and 10 minutes

Servings: 1

Ingredients:

1 loaf

175g (6oz) mushrooms, finely chopped

100g (3½ oz) haricot beans

100g (3½ oz) walnuts, finely chopped

100g (3½ oz) peanuts, finely chopped

1 carrot, finely chopped

3 sticks celery, finely chopped

1 bird's-eye chili, finely chopped

1 red onion, finely chopped

1 egg, beaten

2 cloves of garlic, chopped

2 tablespoons olive oil

2 teaspoons turmeric powder

2 tablespoons soy sauce

4 tablespoons fresh parsley, chopped

100mls (3½ oz) water

60mls (2fl oz) red wine

Directions:

Heat the oil in a pan and add the garlic, chili, carrot, celery, onion, mushrooms and turmeric.

Cook for 5 minutes.

Place the haricot beans in a bowl and stir in the nuts, vegetables, soy sauce, egg, parsley, red wine and water.

Grease and line a large loaf tin with greaseproof paper.

Spoon the mixture into the loaf tin, cover with foil and bake in the oven at 190C/375F for 60-90 minutes.

Let it stand for 10 minutes then turn onto a serving plate.

Nutrition:

Calories: 199

Total Fat: 12 g

Cholesterol: 132.8 mg

Sodium: 168 mg

Potassium: 368 mg

Total Carbohydrates: 16.3 g

Protein: 9 g

Almond Crackers

Preparation time: 15 minutes

Cooking time: 30 minutes

Servings: 40

Ingredients:

40 crackers

1 cup almond flour

¼ teaspoon baking soda

1/8 teaspoon black pepper

3 tablespoons sesame seeds

1 egg, beaten

Salt and pepper to taste

Directions:

Pre-heat your oven to 350 degrees F.

Line two baking sheets with parchment paper and keep them on the side.

Mix the dry ingredients in a large bowl and add egg, mix well and form dough.

Divide dough into two balls.

Roll out the dough between two pieces of parchment paper.

Cut into crackers and transfer them to prepared baking sheet.

Bake for 15-20 minutes.

Repeat until all the dough has been used up.

Leave crackers to cool and serve as needed as a snack or with one or more of the spreads as appetizers.

Nutrition:

Calories: 130

Total Fat: 2 g

Cholesterol:

Sodium: 115 mg

Total Carbohydrates: 24 g

Protein: 3 g

Sweet Bites

Preparation time: 10 minutes

Cooking time: 1 hour

Servings: 15

Ingredients:

120g walnuts

30g dark chocolate (85% cocoa)

250g dates

1 tablespoon pure cocoa powder

1 tablespoon turmeric

1 tablespoon of olive oil

Contents of a vanilla pod or some vanilla flavoring

Directions:

Coarsely crumble the chocolate and mix it with the walnuts in a food processor into a fine powder. Then add the other ingredients and stir until you have uniform dough.

If necessary, add 1 to 2 tablespoons of water.

Form 15 pieces from the mixture and refrigerate in an airtight tin for at least one hour.

The bites will remain in the refrigerator for a week.

Nutrition:

Calories: 210

Total Fat: 14 g

Cholesterol: 10 mg

Sodium: 230 mg

Carbohydrates: 22 g

Protein: 2 g

Cocoa Bars

Preparation time: 20 minutes

Cooking time: 2 hours

Servings: 12

Ingredients:

1 cup unsweetened cocoa chips

2 cups rolled oats

1 cup low-fat peanut butter

½ cup chia seeds

½ cup raisins

¼ cup coconut sugar

½ cup coconut milk

Directions:

Put 1 and ½ cups oats in your blender and pulse well

Transfer the shredded oats to a bowl, add the rest of the oats, cocoa chips, chia seeds, raisins, sugar, and milk and stir really well.

Spread the paste into a square pan, press well, and keep in the fridge for at least 2 hours

Slice into 12 bars and serve or conserve in the fridge.

Nutrition:

Calories: 260

Fat: 21 g

Sodium: 20 mg

Carbohydrates: 14 g

Protein: 4 g

Sirt Diet Snacks and Desserts

By

Lara Middleton

139

Additionally, the information in the following pages is intended only for informational purposes and should thus be thought of as universal. As befitting its nature, it is presented without assurance regarding its prolonged validity or interim quality. Trademarks that are mentioned are done without written consent and can in no way be considered an endorsement from the trademark holder.

Table of Contents

143

Baby Spinach Snack

Preparation time: 10 minutes

Cooking time: 10 minutes

Servings: 1

Ingredients:

2 cups baby spinach, washed

A pinch of black pepper

½ tablespoon olive oil

½ teaspoon garlic powder

Directions:

145

Spread the baby spinach on a lined baking sheet, add oil, black pepper and garlic powder, toss a bit.

Bake at 350 degrees F for 10 minutes, divide into bowls and serve as a snack.

Enjoy!

Nutrition:

Calories: 125

Fat: 4 g

Fiber: 1 g

Carbohydrates: 4 g

Protein: 2 g

Sesame Dip

Preparation time: 10 minutes

Cooking time: 0 minutes

Servings: 1

Ingredients:

1 cup sesame seed paste, pure

Black pepper to the taste

1 cup veggie stock

½ cup lemon juice

½ teaspoon cumin, ground

3 garlic cloves, chopped

Directions:

In your food processor, mix the sesame paste with black pepper, stock, lemon juice, cumin and garlic.

Pulse very well, divide into bowls and serve as a party dip.

Enjoy!

Nutrition:

Calories: 120

Fat: 12 g

Fiber: 2 g

Carbohydrates: 7 g

Protein: 4 g

Rosemary Squash Dip

Preparation time: 10 minutes

Cooking time: 40 minutes

Servings: 1

Ingredients:

1 cup butternut squash, peeled and cubed

1 tablespoon water

Cooking spray

2 tablespoons coconut milk

2 teaspoons rosemary, dried

Black pepper to the taste

Directions:

Spread squash cubes on a lined baking sheet, spray some cooking oil, introduce in the oven, bake at 365 degrees F for 40 minutes.

Transfer to your blender, add water, milk, rosemary and black pepper, pulse well, divide into small bowls and serve.

Enjoy!

Nutrition:

Calories: 182

Fat: 5 g

Fiber: 7 g

Carbohydrates: 12 g

Protein: 5 g

Bean Spread

Preparation time: 10 minutes

Cooking time: 6 hours

Servings: 1

Ingredients:

1 cup white beans, dried

1 teaspoon apple cider vinegar

1 cup veggie stock

1 tablespoon water

Directions:

151

In your slow cooker, mix beans with stock, stir, cover, cook on Low for 6 hours.

Drain and transfer to your food processor, add vinegar and water, pulse well, divide into bowls and serve.

Enjoy!

Nutrition:

Calories: 181

Fat: 6 g

Fiber: 5 g

Carbohydrates: 9 g

Protein: 7 g

Corn Spread

Preparation time: 10 minutes

Cooking time: 10 minutes

Servings: 1

Ingredients:

30 ounces canned corn, drained

2 green onions, chopped

½ cup coconut cream

1 jalapeno, chopped

½ teaspoon chili powder

Directions:

In a small pan, combine the corn with green onions, jalapeno and chili powder, stir, and bring to a simmer.

Cook over medium heat for 10 minutes, leave aside to cool down, add coconut cream, stir well, divide into small bowls and serve as a spread.

Enjoy!

Nutrition:

Calories: 192

Fat: 5

Fiber 10

Carbohydrates: 11 g

Protein: 8 g

Mushroom Dip

Preparation time: 10 minutes

Cooking time: 20 minutes

Servings: 1

Ingredients:

1 cup yellow onion, chopped

3 garlic cloves, minced

1 pound mushrooms, chopped

28 ounces tomato sauce, no-salt-added

Black pepper to the taste

Directions:

Put the onion in a pot, add garlic, mushrooms, black pepper and tomato sauce, and stir.

Cook over medium heat for 20 minutes, leave aside to cool down, divide into small bowls and serve.

Enjoy!

Nutrition:

Calories 215

Fat: 4 g

Fiber: 7 g

Carbohydrates: 3 g

Protein: 7 g

Salsa Bean Dip

Preparation time: 10 minutes

Cooking time: 20 minutes

Servings: 1

Ingredients:

½ cup salsa

2 cups canned white beans, no-salt-added, drained and rinsed

1 cup low-fat cheddar, shredded

2 tablespoons green onions, chopped

Directions:

In a small pot, combine the beans with the green onions and salsa, stir, bring to a simmer over medium heat, and cook for 20 minutes Add cheese, stir until it melts, and take off heat, leave aside to cool down, divide into bowls and serve.

Enjoy!

Nutrition:

Calories: 212

Fat: 5 g

Fiber: 6 g

Carbohydrates: 10 g

Protein: 8 g

Mung Beans Snack Salad

Preparation time: 10 minutes

Cooking time: 0 minutes

Servings: 1

Ingredients:

2 cups tomatoes, chopped

2 cups cucumber, chopped

3 cups mixed greens

2 cups mung beans, sprouted

2 cups clover sprouts

For the salad dressing:

1 tablespoon cumin, ground

1 cup dill, chopped

4 tablespoons lemon juice

159

1 avocado, pitted, peeled and roughly chopped

1 cucumber, roughly chopped

Directions:

In a salad bowl, mix tomatoes with 2 cups cucumber, greens, clover and mung sprout.

In your blender, mix cumin with dill, lemon juice, 1 cucumber and avocado, blend really well, add this to your salad, toss well and serve as a snack

Enjoy!

Nutrition:

Calories: 120

Fat: 0 g

Fiber: 2 g

Carbohydrates: 1 g

Protein: 6 g

Greek Party Dip

Preparation time: 10 minutes

Cooking time: 0 minutes

Servings: 1

Ingredients:

½ cup coconut cream

1 cup fat-free Greek yogurt

2 teaspoons dill, dried

2 teaspoons thyme, dried

1 teaspoon sweet paprika

2 teaspoons no-salt-added sun-dried tomatoes, chopped

2 teaspoons parsley, chopped

2 teaspoons chives, chopped

Black pepper to the taste

Directions:

In a bowl, mix cream with yogurt, dill with thyme, paprika, tomatoes, parsley, chives and pepper, stir well.

Divide into smaller bowls and serve as a dip.

Enjoy!

Nutrition:

Calories: 100

Fat: 1 g

Fiber: 4 g

Carbohydrates: 8 g

Protein: 3 g

Zucchini Bowls

Preparation time: 10 minutes

Cooking time: 20 minutes

Servings: 12

Ingredients:

Cooking spray

½ cup dill, chopped

1 egg

½ cup whole wheat flour

Black pepper to the taste

1 yellow onion, chopped

2 garlic cloves, minced

3 zucchinis, grated

Directions:

163

In a bowl, mix zucchinis with garlic, onion, flour, pepper, egg and dill, stir well, shape small bowls out of this mix.

Arrange them on a lined baking sheet; grease them with some cooking spray.

Bake at 400 degrees F for 20 minutes, flipping them halfway, divide them into bowls and serve as a snack.

Enjoy!

Nutrition:

Calories: 120

Fat: 1 g

Fiber: 4 g

Carbohydrates: 12 g

Protein: 6 g

Baking Powder Biscuits

Preparation time: 10 minutes

Cooking time: 10 minutes

Servings: 1 2

Ingredients:

1 egg white

1 c. white whole-wheat flour

4 tbsp. of Non-hydrogenated vegetable shortening

1 tbsp. sugar

2/3 c. low-fat milk

1 c. unbleached all-purpose flour

4 tsps. Sodium-free baking powder

Directions:

Preheat oven to 450°F. Take out a baking sheet and set aside.

165

Place the flour, sugar, and baking powder into a mixing bowl and whisk well to combine.

Cut the shortening into the mixture using your fingers, and work until it resembles coarse crumbs. Add the egg white and milk and stir to combine.

Turn the dough out onto a lightly floured surface and knead 1 minute. Roll dough to ¾ inch thickness and cut into 12 rounds.

Place rounds on the baking sheet. Place baking sheet on middle rack in oven and bake 10 minutes.

Remove baking sheet and place biscuits on a wire rack to cool.

Nutrition:

Calories: 118

Fat: 4 g

Carbohydrates: 16 g

Protein: 3 g

Sugars: 0.2 g

Sodium: 294 mg

Vegan Rice Pudding

Preparation time: 5 minutes

Cooking time: 20 minutes

Servings: 8

Ingredients:

½ tsp. ground cinnamon

1 c. rinsed basmati

1/8 tsp. ground cardamom

¼ c. sugar

1/8 tsp. pure almond extract

1 quart vanilla nondairy milk

1 tsp. pure vanilla extract

Directions:

Measure all of the ingredients into a saucepan and stir well to combine. Bring to a boil over medium-high heat.

Once boiling, reduce heat to low and simmer, stirring very frequently, about 15–20 minutes.

Remove from heat and cool. Serve sprinkled with additional ground cinnamon if desired.

Nutrition:

Calories: 148

Fat: 2 g

Carbohydrates: 26 g

Protein: 4 g

Sugars: 35 g

Sodium: 150 mg

Orange and Carrots

Preparation time: 5 minutes

Cooking time: 25 minutes

Servings: 1

Ingredients:

1 pound carrots, peeled and roughly sliced

1 yellow onion, chopped

1 tablespoon olive oil

Zest of 1 orange, grated

Juice of 1 orange

1 orange, peeled and cut into segments

1 tablespoon rosemary, chopped

A pinch of salt and black pepper

Directions:

Heat up a pan with the oil over medium-high heat.

Add the onion and sauté for 5 minutes.

Add the carrots, the orange zest and the other ingredients.

Cook over medium heat for 20 minutes more, divide between plates and serve.

Nutrition:

Calories: 140

Fat: 3.9 g

Fiber: 5 g

Carbohydrates: 26.1 g

Protein: 2.1 g

Baked Broccoli and Pine Nuts

Preparation time: 10 minutes

Cooking time: 30 minutes

Servings: 1

Ingredients:

2 tablespoons olive oil

1 pound broccoli florets

1 tablespoon garlic, minced

1 tablespoon pine nuts, toasted

1 tablespoon lemon juice

2 teaspoons mustard

A pinch of salt and black pepper

Directions:

In a roasting pan, combine the broccoli with the oil, the garlic and the other ingredients, toss and bake at 380 degrees F for 30 minutes. Divide everything between plates and serve as snack.

Nutrition:

Calories: 220

Fat: 6 g

Fiber: 2 g

Carbohydrates: 7 g

Protein: 6 g

Turmeric Carrots

Preparation time: 10 minutes

Cooking time: 40 minutes

Servings: 1

Ingredients:

1 pound baby carrots, peeled

1 tablespoon olive oil

2 spring onions, chopped

2 tablespoons balsamic vinegar

2 garlic cloves, minced

1 teaspoon turmeric powder

1 tablespoon chives, chopped

¼ teaspoon cayenne pepper

A pinch of salt and black pepper

Directions:

Spread the carrots on a baking sheet lined with parchment paper, add the oil, the spring onions and the other ingredients, toss and bake at 380 degrees F for 40 minutes.

Divide the carrots between plates and serve.

Nutrition:

Calories: 79

Fat: 3.8 g

Fiber: 3.7 g

Carbohydrates: 10.9 g

Protein: 1 g

Hawaii Salad

Preparation time: 10 minutes

Cooking time: 15 minutes

Servings: 1

Ingredients:

1 hand Arugula

1 / 2 pieces Red onion

1 piece winter carrot

2 pieces Pineapple slices

80 g Diced ham

1 pinch Salt

1 pinch Black pepper

Directions:

Cut the red onion into thin half rings.

Remove the peel and hard core from the pineapple and cut the pulp into thin pieces.

Clean the carrot and use a spiralizer to make strings.

Mix rocket and carrot in a bowl. Spread this over a plate.

Spread the red onion, pineapple and diced ham over the rocket.

Drizzle olive oil and balsamic vinegar on the salad to your taste. Season it with salt and pepper.

Nutrition:

Calories: 150

Total Fat: 2.8 g

Cholesterol: 2 mg

Sodium: 42 mg

Potassium: 172 mg

Carbohydrates: 23 g

Protein: 2 g

Fresh Salad with Orange Dressing

Preparation time: 10 minutes

Cooking time: 15 minutes

Servings: 1

Ingredients:

1 / 2 fruit Salad

1 piece yellow bell pepper

1 piece Red pepper

100 g Carrot (grated)

1 hand Almonds

Dressing:

4 tablespoon Olive oil

110 ml Orange juice (fresh)

1 tablespoon Apple cider vinegar

Directions:

Clean the peppers and cut them into long thin strips.

Tear off the lettuce leaves and cut them into smaller pieces.

Mix the salad with the peppers and the carrots processed in a bowl.

Roughly chop the almonds and sprinkle over the salad.

Mix all the ingredients for the dressing in a bowl.

Pour the dressing over the salad just before serving.

Nutrition:

Calories: 46.6

Total Fat: 0.1 g

Sodium: 230.8 mg

Potassium: 35.6 mg

Total Carbohydrates: 5.6 g

Protein: 0.7 g

Sweet Potato Hash Brown

Preparation time: 5 minutes

Cooking time: 15 minutes

Servings: 2

Ingredients:

1 pinch Celtic sea salt

1 tablespoon Coconut oil

2 pieces Sweet potato

2 pieces Red onion

2 teaspoons Balsamic vinegar

1 piece Apple

125 g lean bacon strips

Directions:

179

Clean the red onions and cut them into half rings.

Heat a pan with a little coconut oil over medium heat. Fry the onion until it's almost done.

Add the balsamic vinegar and a pinch of salt and cook until the balsamic vinegar has boiled down. Put aside.

Peel the sweet potatoes and cut them into approx. 1.5 cm cubes.

Heat the coconut oil in a pan and fry the sweet potato cubes for 10 minutes.

Add the bacon strips for the last 2 minutes and fry them until you're done.

Cut the apple into cubes and add to the sweet potato cubes. Let it roast for a few minutes.

Then add the red onion and stir well.

Spread the sweet potato hash browns on 2 plates.

Nutrition:

Calories: 101

Total Fat: 7 g

Sodium: 5 mg

Potassium: 97 mg

Carbohydrates: 9 g

Protein: 0.8 g

Herby French Fries with Herbs and Avocado Dip

Preparation time: 15 minutes

Cooking time: 35 minutes

Servings: 1

Ingredient:

For the Fries:

1 / 2 pieces Celery

150 g Sweet potato

1 teaspoon dried oregano

1 / 2 teaspoon Dried basil

1 / 2 teaspoon Celtic sea salt

1 teaspoon Black pepper

1 1 / 2 tablespoon Coconut oil (melted)

Baking paper sheet

For the avocado dip:

1 piece Avocado

4 tablespoons Olive oil

1 tablespoon Mustard

1 teaspoon Apple cider vinegar

1 tablespoon Honey

2 cloves Garlic (pressed)

1 teaspoon dried oregano

Directions:

Preheat the oven to 205 ° C.

Peel the celery and sweet potatoes.

Cut the celery and sweet potatoes into (thin) French fries.

Place the French fries in a large bowl and mix with the coconut oil and herbs.

Shake the bowl a few times so that the fries are covered with a layer of the oil and herb mixture.

Place the chips in a layer on a baking sheet lined with baking paper or on a grill rack.

Bake for 25-35 minutes (turn over after half the time) until they have a nice golden brown color and are crispy.

For the avocado dip:

Puree all ingredients evenly with a hand blender or blender.

Nutrition:

Calories: 459

Total Fat: 27 g

Total Carbohydrates: 50 g

Protein: 4 g

Spiced Burger

Preparation time: 20 minutes

Cooking time: 30 minutes

Serving: 1

Ingredients:

Ground beef 250 g

1 clove Garlic

1 teaspoon dried oregano

1 teaspoon Paprika powder

1 / 2 tsp. Caraway ground

Ingredients toppings:

4 pieces Mushrooms

1 piece Little Gem

1 / 4 pieces Zucchini

184

1 / 2 pieces Red onion

1 piece Tomato

Directions:

Squeeze the clove of garlic.

Mix all the ingredients for the burgers in a bowl. Divide the mixture into two halves and crush the halves into hamburgers.

Place the burgers on a plate and put in the fridge for a while.

Cut the zucchini diagonally into 1 cm slices.

Cut the red onion into half rings. Cut the tomato into thin slices and cut the leaves of the Little Gem salad.

Grill the hamburgers on the grill until they're done.

Place the mushrooms next to the burgers and grill on both sides until cooked but firm.

Place the zucchini slices next to it and grill briefly.

Now it's time to build the burger: Place 2 mushrooms on a plate then stack the lettuce, a few slices of zucchini and tomatoes. Then put the burger on top and finally add the red onion.

Nutrition:

Calories: 158

Fat: 8 g

Total Carbohydrates: 17 g

Protein: 3 g

Ganache Squares

Preparation time: 15 minutes

Cooking time: 2 hours and 20 minutes

Servings: 10

Ingredients:

250 ml Coconut milk (can)

1 1/2 tablespoon Coconut oil

100 g Honey

1/2 teaspoon Vanilla extract

350 g pure chocolate (70% cocoa)

1 pinch Salt

2 hands Pecans

Directions:

Place the coconut milk in a saucepan and heat for 5 minutes over medium heat.

Add the vanilla extract, coconut oil and honey and cook for 15 minutes. Add a pinch of salt and stir well.

Break the chocolate into a bowl and pour the hot coconut milk over it. Keep stirring until all of the chocolate has dissolved in the coconut milk.

In the meantime, roughly chop the pecans. Heat a pan without oil and roast the pecans.

Stir the pecans through the ganache.

Let the ganache cool to room temperature. (You may be able to speed this up by placing the bowl in a bowl of cold water.)

Line a baking tin with a sheet of parchment paper. Pour the cooled ganache into it.

Place the ganache in the refrigerator for 2 hours to allow it to harden. When the ganache has hardened, you can take it out of the mold and cut it into the desired shape.

Nutrition:

Calories: 141

Fat: 11 g

Carbohydrates: 9 g

Protein: 1 g

Date Candy

Preparation time: 20 minutes

Cooking time: 3 – 4 hours

Servings: 10

Ingredients:

10 pieces Medjool dates

1 hand Almonds

100 g pure chocolate (70% cocoa)

2 1 / 2 tablespoon Grated coconut

Directions:

Melt chocolate in a water bath.

Roughly chop the almonds.

In the meantime, cut the dates lengthways and take out the core.

190

Fill the resulting cavity with the roughly chopped almonds and close the dates again.

Place the dates on a sheet of parchment paper and pour the melted chocolate over each date.

Sprinkle the grated coconut over the chocolate dates.

Place the dates in the fridge so the chocolate can harden.

Nutrition:

100% joy!

Paleo Bars with Dates and Nuts

Preparation time: 10 minutes

Cooking time: 15 minutes

Servings: 16

Ingredients:

180 g Dates

60 g Almonds

60 g Walnuts

50 g Grated coconut

1 teaspoon Cinnamon

Directions:

Roughly chop the dates and soak them in warm water for 15 minutes.
In the meantime, roughly chop the almonds and walnuts.
Drain the dates.

192

Place the dates with the nuts, coconut and cinnamon in the food processor and mix to an even mass. (But not too long, crispy pieces or nuts make it particularly tasty)

Roll out the mass on 2 baking trays to form an approximately 1 cm thick rectangle.

Cut the rectangle into bars and keep each bar in a piece of parchment paper.

Nutrition:

Calories: 227

Total Fat: 19 g

Sodium: 9 mg

Carbohydrates: 12 g

Protein: 5 g

Hazelnut Balls

Preparation time: 20 minutes

Cooking time: 4 – 5 hours

Servings: 10

Ingredients:

130 g Dates

140 g Hazelnuts

2 tablespoon Cocoa powder

1 / 2 teaspoon Vanilla extract

1 teaspoon Honey

Directions:

Put the hazelnuts in a food processor and grind them until you get hazelnut flour (you can also use ready-made hazelnut flour).

Put the hazelnut flour in a bowl and set aside.

Put the dates in the food processor and grind them until you get a ball.

Add the hazelnut flour, vanilla extract, cocoa and honey and pulse until you get a nice and even mix.

Remove the mixture from the food processor and turn it into beautiful balls.

Store the balls in the fridge.

Nutrition:

Calories: 73

Total Fat: 5 g

Total Carbohydrates: 5 g

Protein: 1 g

Pine and Sunflower Seed Rolls

Preparation time: 20 minutes

Cooking time: 35 minutes

Servings: 10

Ingredients:

120 g Tapioca flour

1 teaspoon Celtic sea salt

4 tablespoon Coconut flour

120 ml Olive oil

120 ml Water (warm)

1 piece Egg (beaten)

150 g Pine nuts (roasted)

150 g Sunflower seeds (roasted)

Baking paper sheet

Directions:

Preheat the oven to 160 ° C.

Put the pine nuts and sunflower seeds in a small bowl and set aside.

Mix the tapioca with the salt and tablespoons of coconut flour in a large bowl. Pour the olive oil and warm water into the mixture.

Add the egg and mix until you get an even texture. If the dough is too thin, add 1 tablespoon of coconut flour at a time until it has the desired consistency.

Wait a few minutes between each addition of the flour so that it can absorb the moisture. The dough should be soft and sticky.

With a wet tablespoon, take tablespoons of batter to make a roll. Put some tapioca flour on your hands so the dough doesn't stick. Fold the dough with your fingertips instead of rolling it in your palms.

Place the roll in the bowl of pine nuts and sunflower seeds and roll it around until covered.

Line a baking sheet with parchment paper. Place the buns on the baking sheet.

Bake in the preheated oven for 35 minutes and serve warm.

Nutrition:

Calories: 163

197

Total Fat: 14 g

Fiber: 3 g

Total Carbohydrates: 6.5 g

Protein: 5 g

Banana Dessert

Preparation time: 5 minutes

Cooking time: 4 minutes

Servings: 2

Ingredients:

2 pieces Banana (ripe)

2 tablespoons pure chocolate (70% cocoa)

2 tablespoons Almond leaves

Directions:

Chop the chocolate finely, cut the banana lengthwise, but not completely, as the banana must serve as a casing for the chocolate. Slightly slide on the banana, spread the finely chopped chocolate and almonds over the bananas.

Fold a kind of boat out of the aluminum foil that supports the banana well, with the cut in the banana facing up.

Place the two packets and grill them for about 4 minutes until the skin is dark.

Nutrition:

Calories: 105

Total Fat: 0.4 g

Sodium: 1.2 mg

Total Carbohydrates: 27 g

Protein: 1.3 g

Fiber: 3 g

Strawberry Popsicles with Chocolate Dip

Preparation time: 20 minutes

Cooking time: 5 – 6 hours

Servings: 4

Ingredients:

125 g Strawberries

80 ml Water

100 g pure chocolate (70% cocoa)

Directions:

Clean the strawberries and cut them into pieces. Puree the strawberries with the water.

Pour the mixture into the Popsicle mold and put it in a skewer.

Place the molds in the freezer so the popsicles can freeze hard.

Once the popsicles are frozen hard, you can melt the chocolate in a water bath.

Dip the popsicles in the melted chocolate mixture.

Nutrition:

Calories: 60

Fiber: 1 g

Sugars: 14 g

Total Carbohydrates: 15 g

Strawberry and Coconut Ice Cream

Preparation time: 20 minutes

Cooking time: 1 hour

Servings: 1

Ingredients:

400 ml Coconut milk (can)

1 hand Strawberries

1 / 2 pieces Lime

3 tablespoons Honey

Directions:

Clean the strawberries and cut them into large pieces.

Grate the lime, 1 teaspoon of lime peel is required. Squeeze the lime.

Put all ingredients in a blender and puree everything evenly.

Pour the mixture into a bowl and put it in the freezer for 1 hour.

Take the mixture out of the freezer and put it in the blender. Mix them well again.

Pour the mixture back into the bowl and freeze it until it is hard.

Before serving; take it out of the freezer about 10 minutes before scooping out the balls.

Nutrition:

Calories: 200

Total Fat: 11 g

Cholesterol: 0 mg

Sodium: 5 mg

Total Carbohydrates: 23 g

Protein: 1 g

Coffee Ice Cream

Preparation time: 15 minutes

Cooking time: 1 hour

Servings: 1

Ingredients:

180 ml Coffee

8 pieces Medjool dates

400 ml Coconut milk (can)

1 teaspoon Vanilla extract

Directions:

Make sure that the coffee has cooled down before using it.

Cut the dates into rough pieces.

Place the dates and coffee in a food processor and mix to an even mass.

Add coconut milk and vanilla and puree evenly.

Pour the mixture into a bowl and put it in the freezer for 1 hour.

Take the mixture out of the freezer and scoop it into the blender.

Pour it back into the bowl and freeze it until it's hard.

When serving; take it out of the freezer a few minutes before scooping ice cream balls with a spoon.

Nutrition:

Calories: 140

Total Fat: 7 g

Cholesterol: 25 mg

Sodium: 35 mg

Carbohydrates: 16 g

Banana Strawberry Milkshake

Preparation time: 10 minutes

Cooking time: 10 minutes

Servings: 1

Ingredients:

2 pieces Banana (frozen)

1 hand Strawberries (frozen)

250 ml Coconut milk (can)

Directions:

Peel the bananas, slice them and place them in a bag or on a tray. Put them in the freezer the night before.

Put all ingredients in the blender and mix to an even milkshake. Spread on the glasses.

Nutrition:

Calories: 110

Total Fat: 1 g

Cholesterol: 5 mg

Sodium: 40 mg

Carbohydrates: 23 g

Sugar: 16 g

Protein: 4 g

Lime and Ginger Green Smoothie

Preparation time: 5 minutes

Cooking time: 5 minutes

Servings: 1

Ingredients:

½ cup dairy free milk

½ cup water

½ teaspoon fresh ginger

½ cup mango chunks

Juice from 1 lime

1 tablespoon dried shredded coconut

1 tablespoon flaxseeds

1 cup spinach

Directions:

Blend together all the ingredients until smooth.

Serve and enjoy!

Nutrition:

Calories 178

Fat 1g

Carbohydrates 7g

Protein 4g

Turmeric Strawberry Green Smoothie

Preparation time: 5 minutes

Cooking time: 5 minutes

Servings: 1

Ingredients:

1 cup kale, stalks removed

1 teaspoon turmeric

1 cup strawberries

½ cup coconut yogurt

6 walnut halves

1 tablespoon raw cacao powder

1-2 mm slice of bird's eye chili

1 cup unsweetened almond milk

1 pitted Medjool date

211

Directions:

Blend together all the ingredients and enjoy immediately!

Be careful how much almond milk you add so you can choose your favorite consistency.

Nutrition:

Calories 180

Fat 2.2g

Carbohydrates 12g

Protein 4g

Sirtfood Wonder Smoothie

Preparation time: 5 minutes

Cooking time: 10 minutes

Servings: 1

Ingredients:

1 cup arugula (rocket)

2 cups organic strawberries or blueberries

1 cup kale

½ teaspoon matcha green tea

Juice of ½ lemon or lime

3 sprigs of parsley

½ cup of watercress

¾ cup of water

Directions:

Add all the ingredients except matcha to a blender and whizz up until very smooth.

Add the matcha green tea powder and give it a final blitz until well mixed.

Nutrition:

Calories 145

Fat 2g

Carbohydrates 7g

Protein 3g

Strawberry Spinach Smoothie

Preparation time: 5 minutes

Cooking time: 5 minutes

Servings: 1

Ingredients:

1 cup whole frozen strawberries

3 cups packed spinach

¼ cup frozen pineapple chunks

1 medium ripe banana, cut into chunks and frozen

1 cup unsweetened milk

1 tablespoon chia seeds

Directions:

Place all the ingredients in a high-powered blender.

215

Blend until smooth.

Enjoy!

Nutrition:

Calories 266

Fat 8g

Carbohydrates 48g

Protein 9g

Berry Turmeric Smoothie

Preparation time: 5 minutes

Cooking time: 5 minutes

Servings: 1

Ingredients:

1 ½ cups frozen mixed berries (blueberries, blackberries and raspberries)

½ teaspoon ground turmeric

2 cups baby spinach

¾ cup unsweetened vanilla almond milk, or milk of choice

½ cup non-fat plain Greek yogurt, or yoghurt of choice

¼ teaspoon ground ginger

2-3 teaspoons honey

3 tablespoons old-fashioned rolled oats

217

Directions:

Place all the ingredients in a high-powered blender.

Blend until smooth.

Taste and adjust sweetness as desired.

Enjoy immediately!

Nutrition:

Calories 151

Fat 2g

Carbohydrates 27g

Protein 8g

Mango Green Smoothie

Preparation time: 3 minutes

Cooking time: 5 minutes

Servings: 1

Ingredients:

1 ½ cups frozen mango pieces

1 cup packed baby spinach leaves

1 ripe banana

¾ cup unsweetened vanilla almond milk

Directions:

Place all the ingredients in a blender.

219

Blend until smooth.

Enjoy!

Nutrition:

Calories 229

Fat 2g

Carbohydrates 72g

Protein 2g

Apple Avocado Smoothie

Preparation time: 5 minutes

Cooking time: 5 minutes

Servings: 1

Ingredients:

2 cups packed spinach

½ medium avocados

1 medium apple, peeled and quartered

½ medium bananas, cut into chunks and frozen

½ cup unsweetened almond milk

1 teaspoon honey

¼ teaspoon ground ginger

Small handful of ice cubes

221

Directions:

In the ordered list, add the almond milk, spinach, avocado, banana, apples, honey, ginger, and ice to a high-powered blender.

Blend until smooth.

Taste and adjust sweetness and spices as desired.

Enjoy immediately!

Nutrition:

Calories 206

Fat 11g

Carbohydrates 15g

Protein 5g

Kale Pineapple Smoothie

Preparation time: 5 minutes

Cooking time: 5 minutes

Servings: 1

Ingredients:

2 cups lightly packed chopped kale leaves, stems removed

¼ cup frozen pineapple pieces

1 frozen medium banana, cut into chunks

¼ cup non-fat Greek yogurt

2 teaspoons honey

¾ cup unsweetened vanilla almond milk, or any milk of choice

2 tablespoons peanut butter, creamy or crunchy

Directions:

Place all the ingredients in a blender.

223

Blend until smooth.

Add more milk as needed to reach desired consistency.

Enjoy immediately!

Nutrition:

Calories 187

Fat 9g

Carbohydrates 27g

Protein 8g

Blueberry Banana Avocado Smoothie

Preparation time: 10 minutes

Cooking time: 10 minutes

Servings: 1

Ingredients:

1 medium ripe banana, peeled

2 cups frozen blueberries

1 cup fresh spinach

1 tablespoon ground flaxseed meal

½ ripe avocados

1 tablespoon almond butter

¼ teaspoon cinnamon

½ cup unsweetened vanilla almond milk

Directions:

Place all the ingredients in your blender in the ordered list: vanilla almond milk, spinach, banana, avocado, blueberries, flaxseed meal, and almond butter.

Blend until smooth.

If you like a thicker smoothie, add a small handful of ice.

Enjoy immediately!

Nutrition:

Calories 298

Fat 14.4g

Carbohydrates 38.1g

Protein 8g

Carrot Smoothie

Preparation time: 10 minutes

Cooking time: 10 minutes

Servings: 1

Ingredients:

1 cup chopped carrots

¼ cup frozen diced pineapple

½ cup frozen sliced banana

¼ teaspoon cinnamon

1 tablespoon flaked coconut

½ cup Greek yogurt

2 tablespoons toasted walnuts

Pinch nutmeg

½ cup unsweetened vanilla almond milk, or milk of choice

For topping:

Shredded carrots, coconut, crushed walnuts

Directions:

Add all the ingredients into a blender.

Blend until smooth.

Enjoy immediately, topped with additional shredded carrots, coconut, and crushed walnuts as desired!

Nutrition:

Calories 279

Fat 6g

Carbohydrates 48g

Protein 7g

Matcha Berry Smoothie

Preparation time: 5 minutes

Cooking time: 5 minutes

Servings: 1

Ingredients:

½ bananas

½-tablespoon matcha powder

1 cup almond milk

1 cup frozen blueberries

¼ teaspoon ground ginger

½ tablespoon chia seeds

¼ teaspoon ground cinnamon

Directions:

In a blender, blend the almond milk, banana, blueberries, matcha powder, chia seeds, cinnamon, and ginger until smooth. Enjoy immediately!

Nutrition:

Calories 212

Fat 5g

Carbohydrates 34g

Protein 8g

Simple Grape Smoothie

Preparation time: 5 minutes

Cooking time: 5 minutes

Servings: 1

Ingredients:

2 cups red seedless grapes

¼ cup grape juice

½ cup plain yogurt

1 cup ice

Directions:

231

Add grape juice to the blender. Then add yogurt and grapes. Add the ice last.

Blend until smooth and enjoy!

Nutrition:

Calories 161

Fat 4g

Carbohydrates 39g

Protein 2g

Ginger Plum Smoothie

Preparation time: 5 minutes

Cooking time: 5 minutes

Servings: 1

Ingredients:

1 ripe plum, fresh or frozen, pitted but not peeled

½ cup plain yogurt

½ cup orange juice, or other fruit juice

1 teaspoon grated fresh ginger

Directions:

Put all the ingredients in a blender and blend until smooth.

233

Serve immediately and enjoy!

Nutrition:

Calories 124

Fat 2g

Carbohydrates 26g

Protein 3g

Kumquat Mango Smoothie

Preparation time: 10 minutes

Cooking time: 5 minutes

Servings: 1

Ingredients:

15 small kumquats

½ mango, peeled and chopped

¾ cup unsweetened almond milk

¼ teaspoon vanilla

½ cup plain yogurt

¼ teaspoon nutmeg

1 tablespoon honey

½ teaspoon ground cinnamon

5 ice cubes

235

Directions:

Cut the kumquats in half and remove any seeds.

Add all the ingredients to a blender and blend until smooth.

Garnish with another sprinkling of cinnamon, if desired.

Enjoy immediately!

Nutrition:

Calories 116

Fat 2g

Carbohydrates 22g

Protein 5g

Cranberry Smoothie

Preparation time: 5 minutes

Cooking time: 5 minutes

Servings: 1

Ingredients:

½ cup frozen cranberries

½ bananas

¼ cup orange juice

¼ cup frozen blueberries

¼ cup low fat Greek yogurt

Directions:

Add all the ingredients to a blender and blend until smooth.

237

Add a little more orange juice if you prefer it a little thinner. Enjoy immediately!

Nutrition:

Calories 165

Fat 1g

Carbohydrates 31g

Protein 8g

Summer Berry Smoothie

Preparation time: 10 minutes

Cooking time: 10 minutes

Servings: 1

Ingredients:

50g (2oz) blueberries

50g (2oz) strawberries

25g (1oz) blackcurrants

25g (1oz) red grapes

1 carrot, peeled

1 orange, peeled

Juice of 1 lime

Directions:

Place all of the ingredients into a blender and cover them with water. Blitz until smooth.

You can also add some crushed ice and a mint leaf to garnish.

Nutrition:

Calories: 110

Fat: 1 g

Carbohydrates: 20 g

Protein: 2 g

Mango, Celery and Ginger Smoothie

Preparation time: 10 minutes

Cooking time: 10 minutes

Servings: 1

Ingredients:

1 stalk of celery

50g (2oz) kale

1 apple, cored

50g (2oz) mango, peeled, de-stoned and chopped

2.5cm (1 inch) chunk of fresh ginger root, peeled and chopped

Directions:

241

Put all the ingredients into a blender with some water and blitz until smooth. Add ice to make your smoothie really refreshing.

Nutrition:

Calories: 92

Fat: 3 g

Carbohydrates: 22 g

Protein: 1 g

Orange, Carrot and Kale Smoothie

Preparation time: 5 minutes

Cooking time: 5 minutes

Servings: 1

Ingredients:

1 carrot, peeled

1 orange, peeled

1 stick of celery

1 apple, cored

50g (2oz) kale

½ teaspoon matcha powder

Directions:

243

Place all of the ingredients into a blender and add in enough water to cover them. Process until smooth, serve and enjoy.

Nutrition:

Calories: 150

Fat: 1 g

Carbohydrates: 36 g

Protein: 4 g

Creamy Strawberry and Cherry Smoothie

Preparation time: 5 minutes

Cooking time: 5 minutes

Servings: 1

Ingredients:

100g (3½ oz) strawberries

75g (3oz) frozen pitted cherries

1 tablespoon plain full-fat yogurt

175mls (6fl oz) unsweetened soya milk

Directions:

Place all of the ingredients into a blender and process until smooth. Serve and enjoy.

Nutrition:

Calories: 135

Fat: 1 g

Carbohydrates: 25 g

Protein: 3 g

Pineapple and Cucumber Smoothie

Preparation time: 5 minutes

Cooking time: 5 minutes

Servings: 1

Ingredients:

50g (2oz) cucumber

1 stalk of celery

2 slices of fresh pineapple

2 sprigs of parsley

½ teaspoon matcha powder

Squeeze of lemon juice

Directions:

Place all of the ingredients into blender with enough water to cover them and blitz until smooth.

Nutrition:

Calories: 125

Fat: 1 g

Carbohydrates: 22 g

Protein: 2 g

Avocado, Celery and Pineapple Smoothie

Preparation time: 5 minutes

Cooking time: 5 minutes

Servings: 1

Ingredients:

50g (2oz) fresh pineapple, peeled and chopped

3 stalks of celery

1 avocado, peeled & de-stoned

1 teaspoon fresh parsley

½ teaspoon matcha powder

Juice of ½ lemons

Directions:

Place all of the ingredients into a blender and add enough water to cover them - process until creamy and smooth.

Nutrition:

Calories: 138

Fat: 2 g

Carbohydrates: 25 g

Protein: 5g

Mango and Rocket (Arugula) Smoothie

Preparation time: 5 minutes

Cooking time: 5 minutes

Servings: 1

Ingredients:

25g (1oz) fresh rocket (arugula)

150g (5oz) fresh mango, peeled, de-stoned and chopped

1 avocado, de-stoned and peeled

½ teaspoon matcha powder

Juice of 1 lime

Directions:

251

Place all of the ingredients into a blender with enough water to cover them and process until smooth. Add a few ice cubes and enjoy.

Nutrition:

Calories: 145

Fat: 2 g

Carbohydrates: 21 g

Protein: 5 g

Strawberry and Citrus Blend

Preparation time: 5 minutes

Cooking time: 5 minutes

Servings: 1

Ingredients:

75g (3oz) strawberries

1 apple, cored

1 orange, peeled

½ avocado, peeled and de-stoned

½ teaspoon matcha powder

Juice of 1 lime

Directions:

253

Place all of the ingredients into a blender with enough water to cover them and process until smooth. Add ice to make it really refreshing.

Nutrition:

Calories: 112

Fat: 2 g

Carbohydrates: 23 g

Protein: 1 g

Orange and Celery Crush

Preparation time: 5 minutes

Cooking time: 5 minutes

Servings: 1

Ingredients:

1 carrot, peeled

3 stalks of celery

1 orange, peeled

½ teaspoon matcha powder

Juice of 1 lime

Directions:

Place all of the ingredients into a blender with enough water to cover them and blitz until smooth. Add crushed ice to make your smoothie really refreshing.

Nutrition:

Calories: 180

Fat: 2 g

Carbohydrates: 25 g

Protein: 3 g

Chocolate, Strawberry and Coconut Crush

Preparation time: 5 minutes

Cooking time: 5 minutes

Servings: 1

Ingredients:

100mls (3½fl oz) coconut milk

100g (3½oz) strawberries

1 banana

1 tablespoon 100% cocoa powder or cacao nibs

1 teaspoon matcha powder

Directions:

Toss all of the ingredients into a blender and process them to a creamy consistency.

Add a little extra water if you need to thin it a little. Add crushed ice to make your smoothie really refreshing.

Nutrition:

Calories: 220

Fat: 3 g

Carbohydrates: 30 g

Protein: 5 g

Banana and Kale Smoothie

Preparation time: 5 minutes

Cooking time: 5 minutes

Servings: 1

Ingredients:

50g (2oz) kale

1 banana

200mls (7fl oz) unsweetened soya milk

Directions:

Place all of the ingredients into a blender with enough water to cover them and process until smooth. Add ice to make it really refreshing.

Nutrition:

Calories: 189

Fat: 2 g

Carbohydrates: 25 g

Protein: 3 g

Cranberry and Kale Crush

Preparation time: 5 minutes

Cooking time: 5 minutes

Servings: 1

Ingredients:

75g (3oz) strawberries

50g (2oz) kale

120mls (4fl oz) unsweetened cranberry juice

1 teaspoon chia seeds

½ teaspoon matcha powder

Directions:

261

Place all of the ingredients into a blender and process until smooth. Add some crushed ice and a mint leaf or two for a really refreshing drink.

Nutrition:

Calories: 213

Fat: 1 g

Carbohydrates: 28 g

Protein: 3 g

Grape, Celery and Parsley Reviver

Preparation time: 5 minutes

Cooking time: 5 minutes

Servings: 1

Ingredients:

75g (3oz) red grapes

3 sticks of celery

1 avocado, de-stoned and peeled

1 tablespoon fresh parsley

½ teaspoon matcha powder

Directions:

Place all of the ingredients into a blender with enough water to cover them and blitz until smooth and creamy. Add crushed ice to make it even more refreshing.

Nutrition:

Calories: 253

Fat: 2 g

Carbohydrates: 35 g

Protein: 3 g

Grapefruit and Celery Blast

Preparation time: 5 minutes

Cooking time: 5 minutes

Servings: 1

Ingredients:

1 grapefruit, peeled

2 stalks of celery

50g (2oz) kale

½ teaspoon matcha powder

Directions:

Place all the ingredients into a blender with enough water to cover them and blitz until smooth.

Add crushed ice to make it even more refreshing.

Nutrition:

Calories: 220

Fat: 1 g

Carbohydrates: 31 g

Protein: 2 g

Tropical Chocolate Delight

Preparation time: 5 minutes

Cooking time: 5 minutes

Servings: 1

Ingredients:

1 mango, peeled & de-stoned

75g (3oz) fresh pineapple, chopped

50g (2oz) kale

25g (1oz) rocket

1 tablespoon 100% cocoa powder or cacao nibs

150mls (5fl oz) coconut milk

Directions:

Place all of the ingredients into a blender and blitz until smooth. You can add a little water if it seems too thick.

Add crushed ice to make it even more refreshing.

Nutrition:

Calories: 289

Fat: 4 g

Carbohydrates: 37 g

Protein: 3 g